"A Change of Seasons"

Poetry Depicting

Life,

Love,

Religion

*Ricky & Shane!
Enjoy & God
Bless.
Love,
Kendall
8/26/01*

Kendall E. Reaves

Published in Flint, MI, by LaBran Publishing.

Scripture quotations are from the King James
Version of the Bible.

Permission has been granted to publish the
names of persons for whom poems were
originally written.

Previously published ISBN-0-9679473-0-8

ISBN 0-9700970-0-X

Printed in United States of America

Dedication

To my loving and devoted Grandparents
Horace and Theola Pea
With my everlasting and undying love
Gram I see you smiling

Acknowledgements

*First and foremost, I thank God, my heavenly Father,
it is only through you that I write.*

*Mom, Brandi, and LaMar thank you for listening to me
constantly, expecially when you all are tired of me.
Brandi allow your voice to be heard. I love you!*

*To all my family I love you too! Harrel I love you too.
Bridgette, Claudeen, Crystal and Stephanie, my girls!
It is with the 4 of U that I "changed seasons". My
extreme gratitude to Rev. and Sis. Greer and the
Mt. Olive Baptist Church, Flint, MI, for your
unconditional love you have given. You have been
instrumental in my growth. Thanks for allowing me
to have my say.*

*To all my Sisters in Christ...Janet, Anna, Pam, Lolanda,
Cathy J., Ms. Jones, Dawnette and Wanda, thanks for
pushing me.*

*To Karen Tipper, also my Sister in Christ, but I'm sure
you were my sister in another life. You are awesome, and
you need to be gettin' paid Girl! Elya you have been a
believer from the start, thank you for sharing your spirit.
Jesse thank you for your quiet understanding. There are
great things in the works for you. Don't stop! Debra and
Theo Starr, thank you for everything. To June for believing
in "As We Step". Scotty, Howard, Glenn, Debra H., Val,
and Simone for bringing the melody to life. Richard Battle
thank you for making me sound good.*

To my folk on the J.O.B. Thank You: Terrie C., Frankie T.,
Raymond Mc., Jethro, and Bernetta, and the list goes on...
Thanks Celeste for allowing me to share with others while
getting our hair done, I hate to see you go, you have been
such a blessing in my life.

To all of you who have pushed me, laughed with me, cried
with me, prayed with me, or gone through any changes
with me, good or bad, you have been my inspiration, and
it is because of you that I write. Sarah you are truly the
one with the vision, much success to you.

To the one sent as my guardian angel: Without you this
would have been only a dream deferred. Thank you, Thank
you, THANK YOU! You are my Champion.

From the bottom of my heart
to the depths of my soul
I thank you all !
Kendall

E-Mail Address:

poetinmotion_1999@yahoo.com

Table of Content

L I F E

"*Funny how life brings different changes*
You start off young, secure and unaware.
As you grow, life can pitch you a few
hard balls."

Cry Baby

Don't worry when I start to cry
Don't sit back ponder and wonder why?
I cry when I'm happy
I cry when I'm sad
I cry at the loving way my cousin looks at her dad

I cried when the Braves won the world series
It doesn't have to be too serious
I cried on my best friend's wedding day
I still get teased in the worst way
I cry when the love making is soooo good
you can bet behind that I'm misunderstood

I cry when my kids are hurting inside
I cry even more when I've found out they've lied.
I cry when someone wins the lottery game
Not even my money
you know that's a shame

Lord, heaven forbid someone I love dies
You know you will see my silent cries
What you'll find out -
and this is only a maybe
All I am is a "BIG CRY BABY"

1

Thirty Something

Waiting for thirty
Boy that was the day!
That's when the mess started my way
My mind was all twisted
from the husband I had
My kids and co-workers
always thought I was mad
Is this the life I've been waiting for?
Well I think thirty-something
should take a back door
waiting for thirty
Boy that was the day!
Now I wish it all would
just go away

2

Burial Suit

So this was the big guy
Couldn't even pick on someone his own size
I wonder if he had a Mother?
Probably didn't want her beat by some brother
And if she was, he was probably there saying,
"Look man, don't you dare touch my Mom, or I'll
have to do you some harm."
Just look at him lying there
Peaceful and all, without a care
Doesn't it just make you mad
Knowing what kind of life he had?
Beating women and having his way
Put him in this casket today
He always thought her fear was cute
But cute put him in his burial suit
I hate it when it comes to this
He never thought she'd really get pissed
She put that bullet right in his brain
And I hope the Judge doesn't claim she was sane
Temporary insanity will be the plea
And she will walk, you wait and see
So come on sister take a stand
Don't put up with the abusive man
Don't kill him, but walk away
Leave him, leave him, leave him today
Look at him, this ain't cute
It could be you in the burial suit

3

Cancer Is Not The Answer

Driving big cars, sailing along
Making big money, doing no wrong
Wife by his side day by day
Living for God, that's the only way
He was going to church, doing God's will
Then he found out he was human still
'Cause one day he started to feel kind of bad
So he went to the doctor to see what he had
After all the tests, the doctor said "Cancer"
He looked down and shook his head
He said, "God are you testing me,
to see if I have the faith of a mustard seed?"
He said, "Cancer's not the answer, it won't get me.
'Cause I have the faith of a mustard seed!"
He wanted to be bitter and somewhat crude
But he was quick to re-adjust his attitude
Cancer is not the answer even though it hurts so
He wasn't down and full of woe
Cancer's not the answer, he wouldn't hear it
he's fighting this thing with a even spirit
Keep praying my friend we're all praying too
We know cancer's not the answer for a great
guy like you.

4

For. *Steve Henderson*

Uncle P. K.

You were always there to rescue us.
Always a smile and a little fuss.
Always there in our time of need,
We didn't have to beg or plead.
The hardest working man in Flint, we know,
working two jobs for fifty years or so.

Then suddenly you started to lose your pace,
But we can rejoice, cause you ran a good race.
And we'll all get comfort in one thing at least,
You're now with God, resting in peace.

The Dad I Never Had

I always wanted to be your pretty brown-eyed girl
Dad you never let me in your world
I wish you'd make me understand
Call, talk to me, be a man

Was it my mother, or was it your wife
That wouldn't allow me in your life?
Was it you didn't know what to do
With this child who needed you?

I could have grown up with the others
There were some sisters and a slew of brothers
You could have taught me things
mother's just don't teach
Why in the world were you so out of reach?

You could have taught me how to deal with men
Maybe I wouldn't be in the shape I'm in
Being with this one, this one and that one
Always looking for that male affection

When I look at my cousins I feel sad
I see how they are with your brothers - their dads
Maybe we can talk if it's not to late
Or do we continue to procrastinate?

Maybe we could even do lunch
And discuss how I feel over lemonade punch
I'm grown up now, and it's time to find out
So I can erase all wonder and doubt

I'll try to keep from being mad
While I talk to . . . .
The Dad I Never Had

6

Looks Can Deceive

You sit there white man with straggled hair
Feet propped up, kicked back in your chair
Lookin' like, any Negro you'd try to scare
But what I'm finding out, you're just a big
Teddy Bear

The people you work with love your style
You tease and joke with them all the while
But what I liked about you, that made my
heart sing
You were wearing a button, of Martin Luther
King

That was so wonderful and made me believe
How much looks truly can deceive.

7

Last Laugh

Why worry about the white man
who's a Nazi, white supremacist or Ku Klux Klan
we better worry about the things at hand
like, you know, our own so called brother man.

You call each other brother, then stab each other
in the back.
Then have the nerve to worry about the white
man's attack.

You know my Black people, this just ain't
right.
Instead of being afraid of them
we're afraid of each other at night.

When we look at our Black Communities
and think of homicide,
we need to re-think that word
'cause it's really genocide.

You're working for the white man every single day
What I mean is.
You're killing each other for them
all done without a cent of pay.

We shouldn't go out like this, stop calling
each other's bluff
'Cause what you don't understand,
white folk love this stuff.

They probably sit back and
laugh as we pull the trigger,
Just fall out laughing on the floor
saying, *"Look at those dumb Niggers"*.

So, I'm pleading to you, my people
on our own behalf.
Don't give the white man this satisfaction
Let us have the last laugh!

Your House

Coming to your house
is like playing in the rain on a
budding spring day,
or babies rolling on the floor
giggling as they play.

Coming to your house
there's an abundance of knowledge
everywhere.
Being at your house/your home
is like a breath of crisp fresh air.

10

Coming to your house
there's always a hearty welcome
and a smile.
This could pose a problem, we may
want to stay a while.

Coming to your house
come, let the truth, be told.
Where do you hide the fountain
for never growing old.

Coming to your house
is like a ray of sun
kittens with yarn having fun
the cat in the hat with
green eggs and ham
I'm telling the truth I am
I am.

Coming to your house
is like unconditional love all
around.
Like, a speaker in every Corner,
you know - Love in surround.

Coming to your house
is like being in a place that
soothes the soul.
We don't know what the secret is
and we'll probably never know.

Oh I know!
Coming to your house
we feel God's earthly presence
and that's the reason coming to
your house/your home
is so very pleasant!

11

My Friend

We've known each other for quite a while
We used to greet each other with, 'hello' and a smile
About fourteen years ago we became real friends
As we waited with child for labor to begin
Our situations were different but that didn't matter
We would talk about life or senseless chit or chatter
I could see things in you others didn't understand
Like for instance why you always wanted
the other color man
To me it didn't matter who lit your spark
Because you were a good person
with a generous heart
When your son was about three you found true love
Only for him to be returned to God above
I hated to see you as you went through tough times
Now we know it's time that heals the mind
You've been there for me more often than not
Always able to talk me out of ludicrous thoughts
I've given you my secrets to keep
Only because there is a loyalty so deep
You'll be my girl until the end
No one could ask for a better friend.

12

For: *Terrie Cantrell*

Colored Girl

She's just a colored girl with red hair
kind of unusual skin so fair
You won't make her uncomfortable
when you stop and stare
She's just a colored girl with red hair

She's just a colored girl with red hair
with freckles and all she has her own flare
You're not sure if she's cute, but she
doesn't care
She's just a colored girl with red hair.

She's just a colored girl with red hair
Men please don't ask something stupid like
"Is it red down there?"
She will verbally tear you apart like a grisly
bear
She's just a colored girl with red hair

But when you get to know this girl with red
hair
You will declare, *"Do you come in a pair?"*
'Cause this kind of girl you don't want to share.

The freckle-faced colored girl with red hair

13

Black Man So Fine

Black Man so fine
Chiseled body of granite
Black Man you are so fine
If only my heart could stand it

Black Man so fine
Intelligent beyond imagination
Black Man you are so fine
I devour your conversation.

Black Man, Black Man, so fine
Your head held high,
Your BAD, bad stride
Black Man you are so fine
Just knowing you're my man I'm
full of pride.

Black Man so fine
Something I'll raise my son to be...
A Black Man so fine
You are/BLACK MAN the epitome.

14

The Sisterhood

There are few times in our lives
We run across women we truly like.
It's so rare that women aren't
gossiping, backbiting, jealous, lying
or stealing!

      Your Man that is. . . .

Seldom can you call a girlfriend
to say hi, share a joke, or a cry.
Without the other thinking, she's
a crybaby, or she must be up to something.

15

And how often do women compliment each other?
Girl that hair cut is fly!
Congratulations on your recent success.
You just really look good these days.

When we find friends we trust and believe in,
hold on to them, hold on for dear life.
Because this is the sisterhood

The Sisterhood
The hood that will never be torn down
and replaced by a freeway called division.

The Sisterhood
A hood where you will find no cracked sidewalks
But if you do there will be immediate repair

The Sisterhood
The hood where we allow no DOGS to run free
No tucking our tails ladies.

16

The Sisterhood
The hood where our grass is always green
and our porch lights shine bright.

The Sisterhood
The hood where we'll always have pride,
and God by our side.

        Love Rules
          The Sisterhood

Old T.V.

Remember the old t.v. sets from back in the day?
Called black and white, but to me they looked gray

Some folks had imagination, 'Cause one day my
cousin said, "Hey look at his jacket I'm sure it is red."

I said, "Boy, how can you tell?" I fell out laughing,
it was funny as hell

Then they tried to add color, funniest thing I ever seen,
transparent plastic in red, blue and green

Remember the hanger rabbit ears for a better
reception? Put on a little foil and add to the deception

And if the knob broke and you couldn't see the wires,
You just turned that bad-boy with a pair of pliers

Remember how the picture would sometimes run
Then someone would beat the t.v. set 'till their hand
was numb?

Then the T.V. Technicians would come to your house
and say, "Excuse me, but you need a new picture tube
today."

Then we'd use the big t.v. as a television stand
to set the little t.v. on ' cause the big one never
ran
Back in the day we thought we were big time,
if we could get 3 stations 12, 5 and 9

Now days you have remotes, cable/the satellite
dish, you can stay on the couch and fulfill your
every wish

'Cause with modern technology, we know we
are big time, instead of three stations we
get 1 - 99

18

I hope the new technology is always here to stay,
But the memories of old will never fade away

Tenor In The Sky

Uncle Leroy had a voice
we'll never forget
You could hear his voice
wherever you'd sit

When he sang a solo
he'd sing with a smile
And when he was finished
you would still hum a while

Now don't be too sad, try
and silence your cries
For now he will sing with
the angels on high

The Lord took him home,
we won't ask why
Just maybe their choir needed
"A Tenor in the Sky"

Written for: Uncle LeRoy

Late Thirty-eight

At late 38
I find myself again at the crossroads
Or shall I call it a fork in the road?
Not knowing what path to take.
Not really wanting to make that choice.
But wanting to stay right there in my comfort zone.

At late 38
I'm tired - tired of starting over.
Tired of malfunctioned relationships
Tired of giving of my self, especially when it's not
good enough.
Tired of being misunderstood.

At late 38
I still can't stand being alone - without that oneness
feeling.
Does it truly exist?
I was beginning to think so, but I was fooled
(thought I was on the right track)

But at late 38, I stand without a track.

Standing Ovation

There are pieces of you around the world
In brilliant hues, magnificent swirls
You have touched the mind of our imagination
Filling our hearts with overwhelming sensation
You make a canvas come alive
with the stroke of a brush
When viewed by the masses
our blood seems to rush
Your tender strokes have made us smile and cry
And your work will live on long after we die.
You're not a young man to say the least
But your youth is released piece after piece
Over the years you have stood the test
And it's only through God you are one of the best
A humble man, and well preserved
This awesome reception you truly deserved
So with glass in hand we offer a toast
To our awesome, amazing, amiable host
You are one of God's greatest creations
And you, deserve a
　　　　　"Standing Ovation"

Written for LaVarne Ross-Artist

21

Dolls of Color

There may be a touch of her wherever you go
In a relatives house, or a doll show
A beautiful woman with a child's imagination
Prompted her to start her delightful creations
You may see dolls similar but there are few others

Beautiful Dolls
Dolls of Color

With child like pride she assembles her dolls
with passion
Giving them wonderful names and one-of-a-kind
fashion
She doesn't take any credit for the things she does
It's given to God almighty above
As she prepares herself for a walk in the kingdom
She's enjoying time on earth like a child's dance of
freedom
So while thanking God we thank her for sharing
with others

These Beautiful Dolls
Dolls of Color

For: Paulette Mayfield

Poetry in Heaven

As I lay here beneath the pulpit
Don't cry for me today
I've done the things I've wanted
to do, said what I wanted to say

Pray all of you who knew me,
hug my family tight
Let them know it was Gods will
and the time was right
Smile when you think of me
and all my little sayings
Now I'll do poetry in heaven
while you're down here praying

23

$$L$$
$$O$$
$$V$$
$$E$$

"*Love is like I-75*
    A runaway Highway through Detroit
        Exit 8 mile, make a
                    Left"

My Transparent Flirt

Man. . . .I think he was flirting with me.
Must be my imagination, it just can't be.
But flirting I can see a mile away.
So I know he flirted with me that day.
But just to make sure I was cool, calm, and collected.
Didn't jump the gun or act affected.
Next time I saw him I wanted to see.
If his flirting was a little more transparent to me.
This time I was certain the vibe was strong.
When it comes to a flirt I'm rarely wrong.
Then I had to inquire that very same day.
"Excuse me, were you sending a flirtatious look
my way?"

He said, "The answer to that is, yes I was".
Oh, I was instantly, mentally intoxicated,
Oh, what a buzz!
I drank a mental cup of coffee (with cream)
until I was sober.
Took deep breaths (meditated)
'til this feeling passed over.
'Cause had I acted on impulse
that would have been bad.
I would have given that brother
everything I had.
I had to be discriminating,
didn't want to get hurt.
By this ingratiating brother,
        "My transparent flirt."

What is this Thing

What is this thing all about ?
This person, who is he?
What is this thing all about?
This person, where did he come from?
What is this thing all about?
This person, his quiet persona.
What is this thing all about?
This person, his smile.
What is this thing all about?
This person, his gift to talk and keep me interested.
What is this thing all about?
This person, his touch.
WHAT IS IT?
You know, this - this thing
What's it all about?
This person, his incredible kiss.
What is this thing all about?
This person, the Love we've made.
Hey my person, What is this thing all about?

25

The Kiss

It's been a long time
Since I felt a kiss run down my spine

Lips so soft yet burning up
Should have pushed you away
Just backed you up.

But a kiss like that you don't run away
Cause you don't get a
"Chillsdownthespinekiss" everyday

Just want you to know
It's been a long time
Since I felt a kiss
run
   down
       my
          spine!

12 Roses

Twelve roses that you gave me
really made my day
I watch them as they open up,
each, in their own way

If each rose could speak to me
I wonder what they'd say?
If they were sitting in the wind
I'd watch them as they sway

27

When I look at my 12 roses
I smile and think of you
'Cause only a special person
would do the things you do.

The beauty will persist
As the roses start to dry
But the memory of 12 roses
will remain and never die.

I've Fallen

I've fallen over and over again
I've fallen
Like a boulder from the side of the mountain
I've fallen
Like an apple from a tree or an orange
I've fallen
Like a baby falling to one knee
I've fallen over and over again
I've fallen
Like a kid off a bike on a warm Wednesday night
I've fallen
Like rain from the sky or hail
I've fallen
Like leaves from a tree or those airplane things
I've fall over and over again
I've fallen
Like off a ladder or up the stairs
Crazy as it may seem
I've fallen
Like ice cream off its cone or a dropped chicken bone
I've fallen over and over again
I've fallen
Head over heels, doing flips, and cartwheels
'Cause this time I've fallen for you!

A Real Man

The tingle in my stomach
The twinkle in your eye
The look on your face
When I begin to cry
This is a magic moment
You'll never understand
'Cause you don't know
How long it took to find. . .
"A Real Man."

29

The Morning

Knot in my stomach, sleep in my eye
The way I feel in the morning as you're rubbing my
thigh
I curl up/move closer, my back against your chest
That's my way of letting you know I need your sweet
caress

Reaching back for your hand stroking each and every
finger
These are the moments I cherish as the morning starts
to linger
I hardly feel you breathing that slow but steady pace
These are the times I'll savor not one moment shall I waste

The serenity that I feel as I go through the day
Transmitted from you - to me this morning as we lay
I thank God for you daily as I kneel and I pray
Thank you Lord, thank you for sending him my way.

Touch My Heart

Touch my heart, can you feel it
The calm and steady beat.
Touch my soul, can you feel it
No longer looking for a retreat.

I'll gladly tear down my wall for you
Lay it brick by brick on the floor.
I'll gladly open my heart to you
Just like a double wide door.

31

Touch my heart, can you feel it
Don't touch then run away.
I'll promise to be your safe haven
Every moment everyday.

Touch my heart, can you feel it
As it almost over flows
I can be your soul mate
As my love continues to grow.

Love Is Something Special

New love, old love, happy love, sad
Do you promise to love me when things are bad

Love doesn't come in a bottle with a guarantee
Sometimes you need a counselor as a referee

Love will wake you up in the middle of the night
Make you toss and turn when things just aren't right

Love can make you bitter and truly, truly, disgusted
Especially when the one you love can't be trusted

But love doesn't have to be like the things I spoke of
When you're filled with the spirit of God above

32

Love can make you sparkle like a star at midnight
Or radiate like the rising sun coming into sight

Love can make you understanding willing to
compromise
Love will make you do some things you wouldn't
do otherwise

Love is something special, it's something you can't
buy
Now tell me why on earth would anyone want to try

Love can be easy, just let the feeling flow
When you open up your heart, the love can only grow

So open up your heart and let the feelings go
God will stand right by your side to catch the overflow

Patiently Waiting Impatiently

I'm patiently waiting impatiently
for things to settle down.
Getting back to some type of normality.
Do you remember me?
I'm patient because I know
we can't help what's going on right now.
Impatient because I don't like it. I miss you.

I'm patiently waiting impatiently for you to call me.
I need to hear your voice.
33   But I have no choice -
but to wait patiently/impatiently.
This is crazy, but I'm sure you understand me.

I'm patiently waiting, impatiently waiting patiently.
Lord!
    This is killing me. . .
                Softly.

I know I will see you soon.
I have patiently waited, impatiently
for that day to come.
Knowing I will see you, be with you,
and touch you, calms me.
But I can hardly wait.
Patiently/Impatiently. I miss you so much.

After I see you, We'll be on track.
For a minute, 'cause the dust
hasn't settled just yet
And it won't be long 'til
I'm patiently waiting impatiently.

What Good Is It

What good is a good poem
If I don't have you there?
So what - about the melody
If you act like you don't care.
What good is it to have people say,
'We think you are the best'
If I don't have you in my secret place
To dance and hollar, "Yes!"
I like the idea of touching
The core of a persons heart
But at home should be where the heart is
Where the touching should always start.
So what good is a good poem
If I don't have you there?
It's only a good poem to me
If I have you there to share.

I Didn't Want to

I didn't want to love you
But I love you because I like you so much
I don't even like liking you
'Cause you make me sick
Sick and tired of this
Because you keep hiding behind scared
And scared ain't never protected nobody.
Hiding behind scared just makes things worst.

I didn't want to love you
But I love you because you are so jive.
I don't even like jive, 'cause jive is just that - JIVE.
Like jive turkey, or you're jiving me
Stop hiding behind jive.
Hiding behind jive ain't never saved nobody.

I didn't want to love you
But you were so smart.
Immediately stole my heart!
Hey - wait, that's my heart.
GIVE IT BACK! You can't play with my heart.
GIVE IT BACK!
I was suppose to be in control of that.

35

I didn't want to love you
Because you were confused.
But confused is just a tool you use
while having your cake and eating it too.
What would you like to drink with that cake?
Oh - never mind,
'Cause you're probably confused about that too.

I didn't want to love you
But I love you 'cause it was easy.
The always seem to please me type easy.
You caressed my mind with the stroke of your voice
You left me no choice.
It was EASY!

You're nothing but an easy confused, scared- smart   36
heart stealing, jive turkey.
I didn't want to love you.
            But I do!

You Amaze Me

I listen to you and I say,
This brother must be crazy!
For years I hung to every word you said
Now it doesn't faze me

How can you suggest what I should do?
How you gonna play me?
Why are you now so concerned
You must be in a daze G!

37

But I was cool I bit my lip,
I even had to praise me!
I tell you man you are something else

You really do amaze me!

Thinking it Through

Sitting here tonight I have thought through my
situation. The past year and a half I have dated a
wonderful man. Who has taught me to love myself.
Who has taught me patience. This man has helped
me to think with a level head. He has also taught
me how to gain self-respect, and how to expect it
from others. To me this man has taught me the real
meaning of love and how to love. Let's not forget he
had been a real teacher of communication. Which is
a talent I have lacked over the years. This man has
listened to me when nobody else would listen. He has
treated me really special.

38

But what we have is no commitment, but an honest and
mutual good faith contract with each other. I feel that
this man is my soul mate. Although I feel all this, I
know there is something deep inside that won't allow
him to let go and love again the way I should be loved
something that won't allow him to be loved like he
should be loved. I know I can't force, and I won't force
it on him.

I am filled with a great compassion, respect, and
moreover gratitude for his presence in my life. In our
talks he has encouraged me to find or look into some of
my callers seriously. This has bothered me for a long
time, and it makes me sad. But I know with what he
has given me, I can now do this with no hard feelings
or regrets. I have love inside to give. What this man
has done is made me a better woman for the next
man. The only catch is, the next man has to treat me
better than this man.

I Don't Want to Play No More

I said I wasn't going to write another poem
about you
But I've got one more , then I'm through
I had to get down the way you pulled me in and
pushed me away
I decided I didn't want to play

Then you had the gall to say
I was the only racing horse
I decided right then to get my jump rope, dolls
and jacks...and play on my own porch

39

You said I got on your nerve 'cause
I spoke of marriage too much
But you're the one who drew me in
with your loving touch

Then, my brother, you'd push me away
Get mad at me 'cause I didn't want to play

You could go on sometimes
wouldn't see me for a week
Then when I'd complain you'd run over,
pacify my body, (bring a gift)
kiss my forehead and cheeks

Na, Na, Na, I didn't want to play
You gotta' come with more than gifts
if you want me to stay

Yeah, I decided other people I should date
You're the one who pushed me out there
Now you want to player - hate?

But now I see the deal
There was a sister in the background
spinning her wheels

Just waiting for the ice to grow thin
So she could maneuver her way
and fall right in

40

She ain't nothing but a friend you would sing
Now you giving her a wedding ring!
What I did was fatten the frog for the snake
Though we had good times you made my
heart ache

You said she would suggest things to do for me
Come on baby can't you see
That witch ain't nothing but a snake in the grass
And both of you can kiss ...!

Well you go on with your brand new life
You, your kids, and your future wife
I quess You could say my feelings are a little sore
But it's all good cause, I couldn't play no more.

Ironic

Isn't it ironic what a stolen kiss will do?
I closed my eyes, and there you were...
I was kissing you!

I know it is ironic, your weren't even in the room
Could it be I closed my eyes and kissed his lips too
soon?

What's even more ironic, you were thinking of me too
'Cause when I settled in/next day
I found a note from you

41

Isn't it ironic our little turn of events
How did your face turn up
It was just a simple kiss.

Could it be I wanted to kiss you all along?
I shake my head - what's the matter with me?
This is coming out so wrong

Isn't it ironic, what tricks the mind will play?
'Cause it was you, I know it's true
I kissed on yesterday!

Married Man

I spoke to you like you were a friend
A true blue brother right to the end
But what I found out, you were one of them
What you are is a married man.

Didn't know at first this attraction, SUCH LIFE
Turned out I knew your kid and your wife
Not only that, I love a wonderful brother
Who would be terribly hurt to learn of another.

But we kept going like no one was there
I think we were starting to have an affair
Long hours at night we would talk on the phone
And seeing each other we knew we were wrong.

I'd say to you, "There's no shame in your game"
But I had to be careful of calling your name
Deep down inside we knew the real deal
We wanted each other and that was for real.

Then one day I saw the bright light
God said to me, "you know wrong from right"
Thanks be to God for coming through
This could have been ruin for me and you.

I've taken this into deep meditation
And decided to stay away from temptation
Stay away from me brother - friend
Cause what you are is one of them.

What you are is a married man.

42

What Are We Going To Do?

Is it just the little things
that keep me wanting you?
Or is it just your pleasant smile
that warms me through and through?
Or could it be I can't resist
your firm but gentle touch?
Maybe it's your kiss,
that keeps me wanting you so much
What is this thing? You must know,
I'm trying to work this out.
Plus, I know you want me too,
this I have no doubt.
But I have a situation
just as well as you
What in the world is going on?
What are we going to do?
I can't keep pretending that it's okay to share
Cause I don't want you touching her or playing
in her hair
Can't we forget the here and now?
Throw caution to the wind?
'Cause you want me, I know it's true
And, I want you, my friend.

43

You Didn't Lie

No you didn't lie
  Yet still you made me believe
  Believe that we could possibly be

No you didn't lie
  Yet I closed my eyes so I couldn't
  hear the stuff you were talking
  out the side of your neck

No you didn't lie
  But you touched me anyway
  Knowing I wanted you only
  Especially when you found out
  I wanted only you

You didn't lie
  You didn't actually hide me
  But then again you did
  How mixed is this message?

No You didn't lie
  To me
  But being dishonest to her is
  a different story
Maybe you're lying to yourself.

44

My Needs

I need a man...to whisper in my ear...taste my
tears...not live in fear of love.
I need a man....whose in control...of his
soul...not in control of mine
I need a man....who can say...let's run
away...we'll find someone for the kids
I need a man...who can make love to me...with
out touching me...and I know he belongs to me.
I need a man....who knows my past...but can get
past it...so forward we may go
I need a man...who loves his family...willing to
include me...willing to love mine
I need a man...that's easy going...to balance my
not so easy going...I can get like that some times
I need a man...that loves kids...not only mine but
his...our future
I need a man...that stands for something...as long
as it's right...but something
I need a man...so I can share...show that I
care...it's not just one sided
I need a man...I can hold...until we grow
old...the golden years.
I need a man....I can read...fulfill his need...they
have needs too
I need a man...who knows for a fact...I've got his
back...cause I know he has mine
I need a man...whose smile can light a room...in
times of gloom...and good times.
I need a man...thinking on his feet....no backs
against the wall...it may tumble

But Mostly...

I need a man who loves Jesus first we'll get
through the worst The Kingdom on our mind.

45

Regina and Howard

Today you two start your lives together
By the look in your eyes, we know it will last forever.
Not only love you've maintained over the years
But a friendship that lasted through joy and tears

When young he thought she was cute and a joy
She thought he was just a nappy-headed boy
Then about six years ago she started to see
Just maybe he is the man for me
They'd be at work playing cards
He thought she was playing hard
She just thought he wasn't ready
For a life with a steady
But still she would be talkin' stuff
He decided one day to call her bluff
"Do I have to do hand-stands to get a date?"
So they went out to dinner, and crab legs they ate

That was the start of their wonderful life
Now as you see they are husband and wife
The Bible says, "let no man put asunder."
      Congratulations
          Enjoy one another.

For: Regina & Howard Keels

46

For
The
Love
Of
Mothers

*"If you birthed a child
adopted a child
fostered a child
grandparented a child
encouraged a child
inspired a child in some way
This is to say GOD Bless you all.
EVERYDAY should be MOTHER'S DAY"*

Who Else?

Who else would change a diaper,
clap when you took your first step, read to
you, kiss a hurt finger, be there for you on
the first day of school, help with homework, and
teach you your prayers?

Who else would allow you to cry on their shoulder
or cry with you, protect you from bullies,
(even when you may have been wrong), teach you
to turn the other cheek and teach you the facts
of life?

Who Else?   *47*

You can call her:
Mother,
        Mom,
                Mommy,
                        Momma,
                                or Ma,

God created Mothers because he knew we would
need them.

The Best

I remember it was just you and me,
,us against the world.
When there was no one else around
we were always each others girl.
You have always been an excellent friend
One on whom I can depend
But I never really got carried away
You were my mother, and you didn't play.

You taught me how to be independent
Said "When you grow up I don't need
no dependents."
You went to work everyday
and instilled the values I have today.

If worried it never seemed to show
But Mama I know life had it's tolls.
Remember the day I crawled in your
lap- crying like a baby?
You said, "If you didn't lose your job
don't cry baby baby."
But it just felt good being held by you
like many years ago.

Each day I have you in my life
my love continues to grow.

I don't think we look alike,
but then again we do.
Even though grown - when I grow up
I want to be just like you.

Then, when I had children,
like a flower you bloomed before my eyes.
I never imagined you as a grandma,
you took me by surprise.
The love I have sees clearly,   *49*
a speak dearly kind of love.
I know I am extremely blessed
by my God above.

Remember one thing Mama,
You'll always be my girl.
You have been the best
Mother in the whole wide world.

For Wilma Mitchell

The Loan

The time has come in our life for change
So many things we must re-arrange
The arrangement we've made will change our
lives forever
But we all know it is for the better

Our son looks at us as if we are traitors
But this is a solution prescribed by the Creator
He's only had a taste of the challenges at hand
But it's his Father who can help him become a man

50

But it's you I admire for your ready acceptance
Because you don't receive this from any step-parent
I think we've developed a reasonable plan
And it wouldn't have materialized without you at
hand

I'm loaning to you my most precious possession
I know you'll take care of him 'cause that's your
profession
So here my friend, I present my soul brother
You'll do a wonderful job as his step-Mother.

For: Stephanie Williams

Good Bye

You were more than just our mother
But a very endearing friend
You laughed with us cried with us
until the very end.

You were the vine, we are the branches
Our children are the fruit
Though we know others care
There will be no substitute.

God took your hand, said to you,
"You have passed the test.
Come with me, come my child
It's time for you to rest."

We can't take anything with us
From this life when we pass
We can't hold on to a loved one
But it's the memories that last.

So Good bye our dear Mother.
You had to answer God's call.
And it was wonderful being loved by you
You'll be missed by one and all.

In dedication to: Mrs. L. Keels &
Mrs. Gladys Burger

51

Quiet

Thoughts

&

Short

Talks

*Remember if you're following Jesus
There are no forks in the road*

Out of the Shell

I'm trying to come out of a shell
A life of four years that have been hell
I've made that step to come out
But I'm stepping out with pieces of doubt
Will I ever be out of that Hell?
I just want to be out of this shell.

Impulsive

Jumpin' the gun
Passion on the run
Running fleeing
Never seeing
The brick wall ahead
BAM!
You're dead!

53

Hard Balls

Funny how life brings different changes
You start off young, secure and unaware.
As you grow, life can pitch you a few
hard balls.

Turbulent Ride

So we've had some good ones
we've had some bad.
There have been happy times
and some sad.
But the thing to do is take a look inside
To see if you've learned anything on this
turbulent ride.

55

8 Mile

Love is like I-75
        A runaway Highway through Detroit
            Exit 8 mile, make a
                    Left

Egotistical

Men are so dog gone egotistical
I just stepped over him
Turned around stuck out
my tongue and said, "now"!

Men are so dog gone egotistical
So one day I stopped
Turned around stuck out
my tongue and kissed his lips
...umm ...umm ...umm
and said, "now"!
Girrrlll...!....

57

Men are so dog gone egotistical

Who Really Exhaled?

She waited

and

HE EXHALED!

Happiness

Let not man determine your happiness
But the Lord Jesus Christ
Men will lead you astray
The Lord Jesus Christ is the only way

Quiet Thought #1

When the funeral's over and the day is done
Don't question God, "Why us O' Lord,
Why did you take our son?"
You know it was His will and
surely it's His way
Just ask Him, "Please give us
strength - give us strength today.

Quiet Thought #2

Remember if you're following Jesus
There are no forks in the road.

Quiet Thought #3

In the road map of life there are no
wrong directions,
as long as you're with Jesus.

Quiet Thought #4

If it seems that no one manufactured a
light for the end of the tunnel, then you
forgot to pray.

63

Change

of

Season

Change of Season

As we step into a coming of age
Getting ready for a new millennium
Did we live our lives to the fullest
Or live it to the minimum?

Look back on how we lived our lives
We all made good and some bad choices
As we step into a coming of age
We hear our mother's voices

The voices that are now so clear
Full of wisdom in every way
We step into a coming of age
Living these voices day by day

64

Together, flowers planted in a pot
We helped each other grow
This year as we come of age
God helped our blossoms glow

It's funny as we come of age
There is no rhyme or reason
We are beautiful blossoms standing tall
Ready for a change of season

For Bridgette, Claudeen, Crystal & Stephanie

RELIGION

"If it seems that no one manufactured a
  light for the end of the tunnel, then you
  forgot to pray."

Religious Flu

Be ye preacher man, deacon or on the trustee
board
He may watch T.V. sermons while talking with
the Lord

But remember one thing sister
a man is still a man
So don't let him prey on you with his praying
hands

He will preach to you, pray to you, quote the
scriptures well
While all along inviting you into his private hell

When you're talking to this brother
remember what is what
When you walk away - look back
he'll be looking at your butt

If you're married to this brother
you better treat this fellow well
or he may get weak for a trip to satan's hell

There's enough going on in this world of sin
So why should we get caught in the Lion's den

Now there's some good brothers in the church,
please don't get me wrong
It's just we should read between the lines as
they sing their tempting song

Now, I understand they're human
We are human too
                "But"
It's our responsibility not to catch
                "The Religious Flu"

65

Forgiveness

Today we'll talk about forgiveness
One of the most difficult things to do
But search within your hearts
The Lord will see you through
With the word of God we must saturate our minds
We'll find that forgiveness gets easier with time
Being a Christian it must be our constant business
To open up our hearts and yield to all forgiveness
So if you practice forgiveness and it becomes habitual
You will find in time forgiveness just comes natural.

66

Thank God

Thank God for all your blessings
He's the reason that you're here
Thank Him for your family and
precious memories so dear.
Thank Him for health, strength and prosperity
and keeping your path clear
You just keep on thanking him
and don't have any fear
The Lord will keep on blessing you
year after year after year.

I Hear You Lord

I hear you Lord, quit tugging at me
Leave me alone Devil just let me be

Hangin' out dancin', swingin' my hips
The smell of Hennesy comin' from my lips
Smokin' cigarettes thinkin' I'm fine
Gettin' down with the brothers anyplace anytime.
There's a voice saying, "There something I want
you to see"
I hear you Lord quit tugging at me.

68

I've been thinking about my life, the stumble/the fall
Sitting back wondering, trying to make sense of it all
Then there's this voice, "Girl forget that, hang with
me."
Go away Devil, leave me alone, let me be.

The struggle is on - which way shall I turn?
Don't know if I'll see heaven, but in Hell I'm sure to
burn.
Lord, I hear you, quit tugging at me!
Leave me alone Devil, just let me be.

I don't like the sound of burning throughout eternity
I need to stop, change my life, see what God can do
for me.

I'm going to Church on Sunday, If they'll let me in
Ask the Lord's forgiveness, Repent for all my sins.
I hear you Lord, keep tugging at me
Save me from that Devil, who refuses to let me be.
Aw, but the Devil will keep working trying to reel me in
Putting stumbling blocks in my path time and time again
I'm praying to you Lord: "Keep tugging at me, keep
tugging at me
Together, we'll fight the Devil so I can be set free."

The Lord has equipped me with a shield of armor for my
breast.
Told me, "Now's the time to fight the Devil
Be brave and stand the test."
I want to live right, live right with all my heart
This is the day the Lord has made, this is where I'll start.

I hear you Lord, keep tugging at me,
Stay away from me Devil, from you
I've been set free.

69

Bench Press

Lord have mercy
Ain't you a mess
Just sittin' around
Doing a bench press

Not lifting weights
Like over your head
But sitting on a pew
All full of lead

70

Let me tell you something sister
stop talking abut Sis. Pettigrew
She can see the gates of heaven
And doing what she gotta do

I say, "What you gonna do?
Just keep on sitting there?"
I say to you soul sister
Don't you dare

I say, get up/get busy
work for the Lord
before it's too late
Fo' you be standing 'round
knocking at the pearly gate

The Lord is coming back
Believe it or not
I'm just giving you bench pressers
Some good food for thought

Now you don't have to listen to me,
'Cause I might make you mad.
But let the Lord Jesus Christ come back
And you're not ready
humph!
You'll wish you had

So all I'm trying to say is
God is handing out His test
So please be ready, don't get caught
Doin' a bench press

Ask Yourself

Before the sun comes up if you die in your sleep
Ask yourself, " The maker would I be ready to meet?"
If shot by a stray bullet on a city street
Ask yourself, "The maker am I ready to meet?"
If in a freak accident and you didn't survive
Ask yourself, "Could I walk by God's side?"
Some illnesses allow time to pray for repentance
To free us from sin as we await the death sentence.
Don't wait for an illness, or a freak accident
This is the time, the time to repent.
Remember God is the providence to keep us steady
So ask yourself..."Am I Ready?"

First Sunday

It's first Sunday Lord, O what a sight
The stately beauties all dressed in white
They sit there all proud with lifted chin
Just waiting patiently for communion to begin
Some say Amen, others nod their heads
To let Pastor know they heard what he said
They are well respected, they've done their work
And quiet as it's kept they run the church
Now you might start to wonder "who is she
talkin' 'bout Lord?"
But many of you know it's the
                    Mother's Board

73

Oh Lord it's first Sunday and there's more dressed
in white
sitting there proud and they have every right
with bowed down heads, or fan in
their hand
They're willing to help and praise God when
they can
They are strong and proud from their hats to
their dress
By now you know they're the
                    Nurses and Deaconess

They open devotion with prayer and a song
They say, "well, Amen, C'mon," to help Pastor along
They have their black suits on, that means communion
today
They assist each other in a blessed way
What would we do without these brothers, Lord
Now you know I'm talking 'bout the
                    Deacons Board

Now you may find these people at a door or
a post
You could even say they're your heavenly host
If you find them standing dressed in blue
and gray
Then it must be first Sunday today
They may take messages and keep order Lord
Now you know this must be the
                    Number 2 Usher Board

Now it's first Sunday, Lord usually quiet
and serene
This is the day the Senior Choir sings
But they've changed their name as they sing
to the sire
No longer Senior but now the
                    Chancellor Choir

Lord I like first Sunday it's kind of quiet to me
It makes me feel like I'm walking closer with
Thee
I like the other Sundays, they're more upbeat
They make you want to stand, clap and stomp
your feet
But there's a difference in how I feel when
I walk away from communion and church on
                    First Sunday

74

Hard Act To Follow

You would have thought it was a
special day the way devotion started out.
The deacons were sending up extreme praise,
even Bro. Kirkland started to shout.

Sista' Evelyn started to testify, how
things were going so good.
But she was quickly interrupted by
screams of joy from Bro. Woods

He went on to say how bad things had been
now they're going quite well.
He quickly gave instruction, "Devil!
Go back to your private hell!"

"You can't beat what God is doing
for me," he went on to say
"He's my savior, my guiding light
He's the truth and the way."

By time he got through there was
nothing to do, the sermon had already
been preached
The way those folk were praising
the Lord, it was obvious they had
been reached.

I was watching pastor as he drank
from his glass, he took a great big
swallow.
He had to be wondering about his
sermon, 'Cause that was a hard
act to follow!

Doer of the Word

There are many roles for Women
working for the Lord
You may be a Cook, Missionary
or on the Mother's Board.

You may be a Prayer Partner,
Counselor, Youth Advisor,
On Pastors Aid, Usher Board, or a
Singer in the Choir.

There are many roles we play.
like teaching Sunday School,
You may be the Evangelist
at the wheel, in the transportation pool.

Maybe you're rather quiet
faithful, meek and poised
But then maybe you're a Musician
eager to make a joyful noise.

You may be on the Visitors
Committee, Superintendent, Clean -up Crew
What ever your role in the Church
the Lord is blessing you.

You may be a Christian Story
Teller, a Writer of Poetry,
What ever your gift, reach the
masses giving God all praise and glory.

Our work in Christ is no mystery
let the truth be told
We are virtuous, women walking
in the spirit being doers of the word.

Are We Ready?

As we ready ourselves for the century to change,
Will we as men serve God or remain the same?
We must question ourselves, are we ready or not?
The clock is ticking, it will not stop.
Are we ready to be a family man?
This is what God had in His plan..
Are ready to have respect for all?
Are we praying to God to prevent our fall?

Are we ready to set examples for our family and
friends?
There will be blessings from God in the end.
So as we ready ourselves for the new millennium
Will we serve God to the fullest or to the minimum?
Study the word, our Bible is a mighty sword
Allow ourselves and our house to serve the Lord.
Our Bible is a providence to keep us steady.
But my question today is,
            "Are We Ready?

Sing Choir Sing

Sing Choir sing,
The Church is on fire
It's all because God
Anointed this Choir.

Y'all broke it down like never
before
Sending highest praises to the
almighty Lord.

Sing y'all sing
In a blessed way
Couldn't wait to get to Church
to hear you today.

Sista' Thea sang her solo, her
voice is heaven sent.
She made us wave our hands
in praise as she sang
"How Excellent."

78

Sing Choir sing
The Church is on fire
And its all because God
Anointed this Choir.

When Y'all sang...
"Late in the midnight hour
God's gonna turn it around!"
The spirit was so high even
Pastor jumped off the ground.

The harder y'all sang
The harder Pastor preached
And from my observation
Every soul had been reached.

Sing Choir Sing
The Church is on fire
And it all because God
Anointed this Choir
Sing, Y'all, Sing!

79

First Lady

Being the First Lady must be hard.
Especially when your husband is a man of God
You always have to share him with somebody
Be it the cook's, other Pastors, or ushers in the lobby
You know a Pastor's work is never done
And generally, you're left behind 'cause the house
you must run
But, it takes a special kind of lady to be a preacher's
wife.
You know he wouldn't be the man he is without you
in his life.
So keep smiling my First Lady
You have my deepest regards.
You're the one who's truly blessed
By our Father, our Lord, and our God

80

For. Mrs. Lois D. Greer

Sharing The Vision

A youthful child at the age of 12
a humble servant of the Lord.
went to his pastor, said, 'I want to preach,"
that's when his vision soared

'What would you preach for?'
his pastor said
He answered "Repentance!
Just like John the Baptist did.'

His pastor was convinced, others found it odd
that a child his age was called by God.
So he went on to preach around the table
until he was thought to be quite stable

Now...he knew there was more to do besides sit
in a pulpit and preach
So missionary work became his passion
there were so many people to reach.

26 years ago he came to Mt. Olive, he still had
his vision in tact.
And as you can see from our surroundings, our
pastor is on the right track.

With a family, six kids, the grands and his
wife
He's as proud as can be
wouldn't trade them for his life.

The 'son's of Mt. Olive, another
accomplishment
Over twenty pastors he has reared
And if you meet them they'll proudly declare
My pastor is Reverend Roy I. Greer

82

We thank God for our blessed emissary
and sharing his vision so clear
We thank you Reverend for all you've done
Congratulations on your 26th year.

*Written for: Rev. Roy I. Greer & Family
        26th Anniversary*

Earth Of The Earth

We came to this earth of the earth,
let's not leave just as we came
Will we be remembered how we lived
our lives, or be just another name?

Will we lay in a coffin an empty
shell, our spirit just a float?
Or will we lay in a coffin an empty
body our spirit with the Holy Ghost?

God put us here to praise his name,
spread His word across the land
If we abide, when our time comes
He'll gently take our hand.

Ashes to ashes dust to dust, as final
as it can be.
Do we live our lives up to God's
standards, so we can live throughout eternity?

Time is short no matter how long we live
Be ye, steadfast in praising His name
We came to this earth of the earth
let's not leave just as we came.

"Therefore my beloved brethren be
ye steadfast, unmoveable, always
abounding in the word of the Lord,
forasmuch as ye know that your
labor is not in vain in the Lord"
                    I Corinthians 15:53

83

You Never Really Know

You never really know a man's heart
until his death is near
People show in droves
with smiles on their faces saying, 'Oh he is so dear."

You never really know a person's heart
until that person dies
The tears they've shed
joy they've spread to other people's lives.

84

You never really think about life
until a person dies
How life began and how we live
how time just seems to fly.

So live your life to the fullest
giving God the highest praise
Cause you know from life's experiences
we only have numbered days.

If changes need to be made in life
then let those changes show
We play like we have forever to live
But guess what -
        We never really know!

Games of Life

Peace be still, stop - meditate
Ward off thoughts of scandal and hate
The world will pull you into its troubles and strife
When you're playing the games
         The Games of Life

The games of life, let me explain
Some of the components incorporated in the game.
Babies with guns, teen pregnancies, and drugs
Street educated, jails full of thugs
You're not safe day, night, boulevard or alley
Bullets flying everywhere, drive by shooting galleries
The games of life what a shame
How so many ignore the rules of the game
You can't play the game without the root of all evil
Don't look confused/ I'm talkin' money people
People who worship the all mighty dollar
Will find a noose tighter than a collar.
Then you gamble with sex like Russian roulette
When true love is discovered, you fear a blood check
It really doesn't matter if you're black or white.
"Aw, Na" you're all pawns in the game
         The Games of Life

May I suggest, read your Bible, find out what's inside
Study, obey the Word, use the scriptures as your guide.
God's Word is real, a mighty, mighty sword
Use it to eliminate your current game board
Just remember time is short
In the tunnel a dim light
You may not have time to change the way you play
         The Games of Life

LaBran Publishing
P.O. Box # 4036
Flint, Michigan 48504

Website: www.poet-n-motion.faithweb.com

Cover Design: Roni Lane at Kendall Printing,
Flint, Michigan

Photo by: James Wells - Flint, Michigan